# FX

# FX

*A Day Trader's Guide to the Foreign Exchange Market*

## By: Frank Roche

Printed and bound in the USA

FX: A Day Trader's Guide to the Foreign Exchange Market
**ISBN-13: 978-1483916286**
**ISBN-10: 1483916286**

# Table of Contents

## Chapter 1

Introduction........................................................................... 1

## Chapter 2

Foreign Exchange (FX) since Bretton Woods........................... 5

Bretton Woods, One Last Try at a Fixed System ................. 6

Floating Rates Replace Fixed Rates ..................................... 8

## Chapter 3

Foreign Exchange (FX) Rate Determination.......................... 14

Fundamental Analysis......................................................... 14

Technical Analysis ............................................................. 18

## Chapter 4

The Foreign Exchange (FX) Market at Work.......................... 20

Tools of the Trade............................................................. 22

Spot................................................................................. 24

Forwards.......................................................................... 27

Futures............................................................................. 29

Options ............................................................................ 30

Price Spreads ................................................................... 31

Buy & Sell | Long & Short ................................................. 32

Market Orders ................................................................. 34

Daily Preparation ................................................ 37

Retail FX ............................................................ 38

**Chapter 5**

FX Risk Management ........................................... 40

**Chapter 6**

How to Trade FX ................................................. 44

**Chapter 7**

*Language of the Foreign Exchange (FX) Market*.................... 48

**Chapter 8**

*U.S. Economic Indicators* ....................................... 61

**Index**

**References**

# Chapter 1

## Introduction

Trading and investing in stocks and bonds is not uncommon among those who actively manage their own personal finances. Trading and investing in the foreign exchange (FX) market is far less common. In fact, very few of America's leading financial advisory firms even offer foreign exchange as an asset class in which to invest.

It is somewhat understandable. Media coverage of stocks and bonds is much more widespread than that of FX. International economic and financial news is not covered as broadly as U.S. economic and financial news. Plus, the exotic perception of the FX market, coupled with a comparatively high risk reputation, combined with apparent complexity, scares many investors and personal money managers away.

Investors are missing out. The perceptions are overblown. Investing in the currency market can be very rewarding. Today investors can get involved via the futures market, ETF's, mutual funds, hedge funds, and by directly trading the cash market from a home office. Day trading FX can be an excellent way to boost annual returns, or depending on one's personality and risk tolerance, a good way to make a living.

Anyone with a basic understanding of investing, some understanding of economics, a high degree of, shall we say intestinal fortitude, an ability to perform multiple tasks in a fast paced environment, and excess savings with which to open a trading account should consider day trading the FX market. There are many Internet-based FX brokers offering as much as 50:1 leverage. There are even brokers who allow customers to trade off their capital requiring smaller initial margin funding.

The basic concept for trading FX is not unusual: buy low sell high, or sell high and buy low. Of course, this is foreign exchange so selling one currency means buying another, and vice versa.

In FX there are dozens of currency pairs from which to choose. The currency pairs traded most widely include the Euro against the U.S. Dollar (EUR/USD), the U.S. Dollar against the Japanese Yen (USD/JPY), and the Euro against the Japanese Yen (EUR/JPY). There is a currency pair for every risk tolerance.

While it takes years to become an FX pro, there are some basics that can be learned that will allow for anyone to quickly get started day trading currencies. To aid in that quick start, an FX day trader needs to know what foreign exchange is. They need to know some history of the FX market. They need to know the basics of exchange rate determination. They need to know the different types of transactions, how currencies are quoted, and how the market works. They need to know some basics of risk management. They need to know some of the language of the FX market, and they'll need to know the important economic indicators to watch each month for the U.S. economy.

This book will help the individual investor get started in becoming an FX day trader. Day trading FX will diversify your portfolio and can sharply boost annual returns.

*Warning: The FX market is risky. An investor can lose all of their invested capital. Only invest what you are willing to lose.*

So, foreign exchange, what is it? We can generally think of foreign exchange as referring to bank holdings of foreign currency payable across borders.

Cross-border financial transactions related to trade in goods and services, and capital flows are the catalyst for foreign exchange transactions. If a U.S. exporter sells a product to a Japanese buyer, to finalize the deal the Yen which the Japanese buyer uses will have to be exchanged for U.S. Dollars, the currency used by the U.S. exporter. Or, if a European bank wants to place excess reserves in U.S. Dollars rather than in their own domestic currency, the Euro, they have to buy dollars and sell Euro's.

For a country's currency to be considered foreign exchange, to be part of an FX system, a currency must be convertible. A currency is considered convertible if the holder can freely convert it: exchange it for another currency. Under the heading of convertibility, there is free and open convertibility, and partial convertibility. The U.S. Dollar for example is fully convertible whether the holder is a resident in the United States or somewhere overseas, and regardless of whether any merchandise or financial transactions are involved (SBC, 1992).

Many developing countries allow only nonresident convertibility in an effort to control foreign exchange reserves and prevent the export of capital. At the time of this writing the monetary authorities of the eastern Mediterranean island nation of Cyprus are putting in place currency convertibility restrictions in hopes of avoiding the final collapse of their basically insolvent banks, and massive capital flight out of the country.

Additionally, many countries have differing foreign exchange conversion regulations depending on whether or not FX reserves come from trade in goods and services, or from capital flows (speculative money flows sometimes called "hot money"). Typically the later is more regulated than the former.

Foreign exchange as we know it today began to take shape in the late 1880's. The industrial revolution helped shrink the world with advances in transportation and communication technologies. Cross-border capital flows around the world have been increasing ever since.

# Chapter 2

## Foreign Exchange (FX) since Bretton Woods

By the early 1890s' a monetary system using gold alone as its basis was gaining strength around the world. This effort at a new monetary system displaced a monetary system established in 1865 by four countries (Switzerland, France, Belgium, and Italy). As confidence in this new monetary system grew, it led to the regular practice of settling cross-border payments with strokes of the accountant's pen rather than the actual physical transfer of gold and silver. With the widespread use of new communication methods like the telephone and telex, expanding technology as always played a role in the relative success of this new monetary system. These new communications technologies combined with new accounting methodologies, aided in bringing about the creation of the foreign exchange market managed by professionals.

There have been three post U.S. Civil War efforts at establishing a gold standard for the world's trading nations. A gold standard is a system of fixed exchange rates set in relation to the price of gold. The first called the gold specie standard came and went around the turn of the 20th Century. The second, called a gold bullion standard, followed in the early 1890's, and failed by the start of WWI. Inherent inefficiencies and widespread non-compliance to parity rates by member nations doomed both efforts.

From 1914 to 1943 the economic chaos from war and the Great Depression brought about currency manipulation, international capital controls, varied levels of inflation and interest rates among the world's trading nations, and severe external imbalances. The fixed exchange rate systems were not working.

## *Bretton Woods, One Last Try at a Fixed System*

Armed with a new determination to establish a new global financial system, in 1943 the USA and Great Britain took the first steps towards creating a free and stable international monetary system. The 1944 Bretton Woods Conference in New Hampshire resulted in the acceptance of an American proposal for a quasi-gold standard. It would be another effort at a fixed exchange rate system. The goal of the Bretton Woods Agreement was to establish an international monetary system with stable and manageable exchange rates, reduce or eliminate exchange controls, and ensure the convertibility of all member country currencies.

As part of this new system, the International Monetary Fund (IMF) was created. The IMF would be tasked with monitoring the operation of the new exchange rate system based on the price of gold. Each IMF member state was required to set a price for their currency relative to gold or the value of the U.S. Dollar. As always, members agreed to keep fluctuations of their currency within an established parity price through the utilization of central bank open market operations. Once established, to avoid unwanted devaluations, the rate of any currency could only be modified with IMF board approval.

To discourage countries with current account deficits from the tried and true practice of imposing exchange rate devaluations, and/or capital restrictions, the IMF set up a fund to assist them. Countries with insufficient FX reserves to maintain their parity rate could tap this new fund to help minimize the negative impact on their domestic economy from the necessary economic adjustments required to restore international balance. The amount of reserves available to members would depend on growth rates as measured by GDP, the level of currency reserves, and a country's international trade balance.

Coming out of WWII, European and some Asian nations, crippled by war and constrained by limited FX reserves, could not comply to the new international system adopted at Bretton Woods very quickly. It was done slowly. It turned out to be too slow. The gold standard dreaded devaluations began again.

By the mid 1950's relative calm emerged as the world was rebuilding from WWII. Although, by the late 1950's pressures on some European countries like France re-emerged and forced the French authorities to introduce a new, devalued, French Franc.

Come the 1960's, economic turmoil returned and challenged the structure of the Bretton Woods agreement. The massive flow of U.S. Dollars to Europe for reconstruction, and to Asia related to the Korean War, and the beginning of the U.S. role in Vietnam, brought about significant external deficits for the U.S. economy. These imbalances, both in terms of trade and capital flows put upward pressure on gold prices, and gold spiked above $35. The new spike in the price of gold and continued volatility forced concerted global central bank interventions to stabilize and manage the price of gold.

Disruptions to the monetary system also came from the impact of differing output among countries coming out of WWII. In 1961 the Deutsch Mark and the Dutch Guilder were revalued as a result of large current account surpluses. Yet, from 1963 onwards the British Pound (GBP) remained under increasing selling pressure and was devalued in 1967. This again brought about a run on gold. Huge losses for central banks forced an end to the concerted effort to stabilize the market.

By 1968 the French economy was in trouble again draining away the reserves of the French central bank. For the second time in ten years the French Franc was again devalued in 1969. Huge capital flows into Germany caused problems for the Bundesbank, Germany's central bank. The Deutsche Mark was revalued again in the fall of 1969.

The Bretton Woods agreement was not able to survive for long. Finally, geo-political and economic crises, and then energy disruptions helped bring about the end of the last and most recent effort to establish a global fixed exchange rate system based on the price of gold.

## *Floating Rates Replace Fixed Rates*

By the 1970's the problems plaguing the international monetary system established in the 1940's were too far along to be cured by isolated rate changes. The loss of confidence in the U.S. Dollar resulting from poor economic performance since the late 1960's, and a massive current account deficit helped end the Bretton Woods system of fixed exchange rates.

In the early 1970's lower interest rates in the U.S., a strong rise in the U.S. current account deficit, war in the Mideast along with an Arab oil embargo, and a spike in energy prices across America and the world, set in motion a U.S. Dollar sell-off. As global interest rate spreads widened, it wasn't long before capital flight out of the U.S. was underway with the lions share flowing to Europe, where interest rates had remained high. The capital flight to Europe forced market interventions by the German Bundesbank and the Swiss National Bank (SNB) in an effort to combat their respective currency strength.

As the U.S. Dollar crisis continued, like pouring gas on a fire, the U.S. Congress, in all their wisdom, publically expressed concerns about the challenge of continuing the convertibility of the U.S. Dollar into gold. Not surprisingly, a new flight from the U.S. Dollar began which in a matter of days grew to the many billions of dollars. In August 1971 the United States abandoned dollar-gold convertibility. This breach gave the green light to other nations, tired of the administrative task of compliance with the Bretton Woods Agreement, to abandon gold convertibility as well (SBC, 1992).

With the U.S. prepared to devalue the U.S. Dollar, and Japan and the Western European nations willing to revalue their currencies, a new agreement was struck amongst major nations: the Smithsonian Agreement so named at a monetary conference in late 1971. The USA agreed to raise the official gold price from $35 to $38 per ounce. In concert with the U.S. move, Japan and the Western European countries agreed to revalue their currencies. Like prior monetary agreements, there were requirements for central banks to maintain their currency rates within the established price range (SBC, 1992).

However, pressures on weak currencies continued. Differential growth rates and economic performance between Western Europe and Japan vs. the U.S. and Great Britain, continued to cause large capital movements seeking the highest return with the lowest risk. By the spring of 1973 Japan and Germany no longer complied with their obligations under the Smithsonian Agreement to maintain their currency parity, and the last gasp of an international fixed exchange rate system was heard.

Since the day President Nixon abandoned gold convertibility in August, 1971, there has existed a mix of fixed and floating exchange rates across the globe. Most of the developed countries who claim to have a "floating" currency, have in fact practiced some form of a "managed" floating exchange rate system. This activity has been also been termed a dirty float: central bank intervention in the FX market to favorably adjust exchange rate.

More than a dozen European countries, led by Germany and France, began putting in place the mechanism for a currency union with internal fixed rates, and external floating rates. Today, that is the Euro currency. And today at the time of this writing, because of differing inflation and interest rate levels within the Euro area, combined with differing fiscal policies, the Euro currency (EUR) is at risk of breaking apart.

Many developing countries, most importantly China, have kept fixed rates to the U.S. Dollar, or a basket of currencies like the Special Drawing Rights (the currency of central banks). For those countries that do fix their exchange rate, there is increased use of a crawling peg: a method of regular fixing adjustments based on the developing country's improving competitiveness. China's management of their currency fix to the U.S. Dollar is the best example of a crawling peg. China manipulates their currency on a daily basis to benefit exports from China.

Throughout the 1970's the value of the U.S. Dollar against other major currencies showed a significant downward trend in the new floating system. From 1977 to 1978 the U.S. Dollar suffered another sharp drop in value across the board. The reasons for the second dollar crisis in a decade were the growing trade and savings imbalances between the U.S. and most of the rest of the world, the second of two oil price shocks coming out of the Middle East, and a general drop in investor confidence related to U.S. assets.

The U.S. was not alone, by 1978 the currencies of the weaker economies in Europe like the British pound (GBP), and the Italian Lira weakened further. Not surprisingly, during this same period the currencies of Europe's healthier northern economies like the Swiss Franc, and the Deutsch Mark grew even stronger.

The change in the conduct of U.S. monetary policy under Paul Volker in the early 1980's resulted in high interest rates and a stronger U.S. Dollar as a result of significant interest rate differentials globally. By 1985 the U.S. Dollar had reached a 9-year high causing problems for U.S. manufacturers and employment as U.S. exports dropped and imports rose. The Plaza Agreement, agreed to by the Group of Five (G5) (the U.S., Great Britain, France, West Germany, and Japan) was signed. The agreement called for a significant devaluation of the U.S. Dollar to correct historic trade imbalances between the U.S. and most of her trading partners, in particular Germany and Japan. By late 1987, the U.S. Dollar was sharply lower against the Deutsche Mark, the Japanese Yen, and the Swiss Franc.

In the face of the huge devaluation of the U.S. Dollar, in 1987 the Group of Seven (G7) (U.S., Great Britain, France, West Germany, Japan, and Canada) met and came up with the Louvre Accord. This latest agreement reaffirmed the group's commitment to cooperate closely in stabilizing the prevailing exchange rates. The U.S. Dollar remained under pressure.

Under a system of floating exchange rates it was expected that, after an initial period of adjustment, equilibrium rates would be reached and that thereafter exchange rate changes would occur without major disruption. This expectation has proven false. The fundamental economic factors of growth, inflation, and interest rates have differed markedly from one country to another (SBC, 1992).

Since the early 1990's significant volatility has remained in the FX market. Repeated currency crises have occurred among emerging market countries, and central bank currency interventions have been deemed necessary on a regular basis. The 1997 Asian currency crises centered on Thailand's currency the Thai Baht, and the challenge the Thai central bank faced in keeping the Baht pegged to the U.S. Dollar. Thailand suffered serious domestic and international imbalances, and internal political instability. South Korea, Malaysia, Indonesia, and even Japan felt the impacts in the currency market.

By the mid-2000's another fixed exchange rate system was, and has been in crisis: the Euro zone. Again, faced with weak internal politics, dramatic fiscal imbalances, and an increasingly uncompetitive industrial sector in relation to the rest of the industrialized world, market forces are causing significant volatility for the Euro, forcing weaker member nations like Greece and Cyprus to reconsider their continued participation in the fixed exchange rate system. And, as recently as 2012, the Bank of Japan, Japan's central bank, intervened in the FX market to devalue their currency against the U.S. Dollar in order to maintain their export competitiveness.

Continuing volatile moves in exchange rate relationships should not be surprising and are likely to continue.

A real stabilization of FX rates can only be achieved by a harmonization of international economic policy, global political governance, and a one-currency world. This potential outcome is still a long way off, if at all (SBC, 1992). Although, the currency for the one-currency world has already been established in the utopian hope that world can come about sooner rather than later. The currency is the Special Drawing Rights (SDR), a supplementary basket of foreign exchange reserves. It is the currency of central banks. SDRs are allocated to member countries by decision of the IMF's Board of Governors.

The SDR gives its holder the right to purchase foreign exchange from the central bank or monetary authorities of another member country. When a country is confronted with external imbalances, it can exchange its SDRs for a currency specified by the IMF without any special economic policy conditions attached.

Today the SDR basket of currencies is a trade weighted average of 5 currencies:

| Currency | % |
|---|---|
| U.S. Dollar (USD) | 43% |
| Euro (EUR) | 37% |
| British Pound (GBP) | 11% |
| Japanese Yen (JPY) | 8% |

The value of the SDR is determined daily based on the values of the five basket currencies. It is quoted by the IMF for a large number of currencies.

"Some countries make their first economic priority price stability" (SBC, 1992, p. 23). Other countries put the emphasis on national growth rates or employment. Some, like the U.S., attempt to do both. Because of this, external imbalances among nations will continue. The flexible exchange rate system provides for this and has great benefits: most importantly, the benefit of greater freedom in the conduct of domestic monetary policy. Once central banks were freed from the duty of holding the exchange rates of their domestic currencies within the required margin of fluctuation related to the price of gold, there was no longer any need for daily buying and selling. As importantly, floating rates also eliminated the need for daily sterilization operations to avoid expansion or a contraction of the domestic money supply resulting from the buying and selling of foreign currencies.

Multinational corporations are at the forefront of the push towards a single currency. Libertarian groups around the globe are pushing for a return to a fixed exchange rate system based on the price of gold. Multinationals are motivated by financial risks and administrative costs associated with managing foreign exchange exposure, and libertarians are motivated by a concern over inflation. With the world's largest manufacturing base, China, operating with a fixed exchange rate system by pegging their currency to the U.S. Dollar, and getting rich off of the mercantilist nature of the policy, the push for a single currency gains strength, and efforts to reduce volatility in exchange rate movements continues.

Economists have long said foreign exchange is a result of the coincident rise of international trade and nationalist attachments to national currencies. This will certainly remain the case if or until such time as a single global currency comes into existence.

# Chapter 3

## Foreign Exchange (FX) Rate Determination

FX rates change second by second, 24 hours per day, 5 days a week. The day-to-day catalysts for exchanges rate movements come from a myriad of variables. These variables include: basic supply and demand, monetary policy, fiscal policy, inflation rates, expectations of future interest rate movements, unexpected geo-political events, natural disasters, reactions to economic data releases that don't meet expectations, central bank intervention and quantitative easing, fear, greed, a country's balance of payments, and the sentiment of market participants.

The FX market is an instant discounting mechanism of new information. This is why it is so important for the successful day trader at home to keep a careful watch on headlines, economic data, and other financial market price information. In the end, new information must be analyzed for how it will impact the conduct of monetary policy, and therefore the level of inflation and output for the U.S. economy.

Analysis of exchange rate determination is done based on fundamental or technical data and information.

### *Fundamental Analysis*

Fundamental analysis implies that a country's currency has an equilibrium level that is determined by economic indicators revealed in data published monthly.

While actual equilibrium is rarely achieved anywhere in economics, under a system of floating exchange rates, rates should be impacted primarily by differing inflation rates, and so therefore by the

14

differing levels of interest rates between countries. The real exchange rate, the nominal rate adjusted for inflation is the key metric. An increase in a country's real exchange rate suggests that domestic goods are becoming more expensive relative to foreign goods, which will tend to reduce the country's exports and increase imports. Conversely, a decline in the real exchange rate tends to increase exports and decrease imports.

Nominal exchange rates are, in theory, primarily determined by the economic concept of Purchasing Power Parity (PPP) – the Law of One Price. This theory suggests that an internationally traded product sold in two different countries should cost the same when adjusted by the exchange rate. McDonald's Big Mac is one of the best product examples to use because it is uniformly made all over the globe.

A Big Mac in the U.S. that costs $3.00 should in theory cost 280 Yen in Japan based on today's exchange rate of 93.30 Yen per U.S. Dollar. Of course, this simple example doesn't cover all costs associated with making a Big Mac. The price of a Big Mac purchased in Roppongi, Tokyo, Japan will be more expensive on an exchange adjusted basis than a Big Mac purchased in Sanford, North Carolina. However, it is more closely comparable with a Big Mac purchased in midtown Manhattan.

PPP has a reasonably good record of accuracy in explaining long-term exchange rate movements, although there are some deficiencies. First, differing price indices used to measure inflation and purchasing power result in differing conclusions. Second, only prices related to trade in goods and services are included in the PPP calculation, although there are many more prices in an economy. Third, competition among global multinationals is not just about price but also about quality, shipping time, and support. Lastly, the PPP theory does not account for the impact on FX rates from cross-border capital - hot money - flows. (SBC, 1992)

Whether the focus is on real or nominal exchange rates, countries with relatively high inflation rates have, and will continue to experience depreciation of their currencies, and vice versa.

Apart from interest and inflation rate levels for a given country, and the 20 plus important economic indicators that determine the value of the U.S. Dollar at any time, another important long-term fundamental economic variable is a country's balance of payments. The balance of payments is the sum of a country's current account and capital account, and should equal zero.

The current account balance measures net exports in goods and services, plus net earnings on overseas investments, plus cash transfers. The current account is thought to be a reasonably good measure of a country's global competitiveness. In the long run, a current account surplus will tend to make the country's currency stronger, and a current account deficit will tend to make the country's currency weaker.

The capital account measures a country's net export position of financial capital, including the central bank's foreign exchange reserves. Capital movements, hot money flows, usually dominate daily trading on the foreign exchange market. Fluctuations in the capital account can play an important short and long-term role in determining a currency's fundamental soundness. In fact, one of the important economic indicators released each month which receives a good deal of attention is the Treasury International Capital flow data; TIC data. It measures the monthly net investment appetite on the part of foreign nationals for U.S. Treasury debt, U.S. Agency debt, and U.S. corporate debt.

Foreign currency flows are motivated by trade in goods and services (current account), and flows of financial capital (capital account) seeking out the highest returns among a variety of financial products in places like New York, Hong Kong, Tokyo, and London.

A careful analysis of a wide variety of economic indicators reveals the attractiveness of the investment possibilities in a given country. A country's relative level of interest rates at any given time is critically important in FX. Understandably, capital has a tendency to flow where the risk adjusted return on capital is the highest. The decision to invest in a particular country or not should be based on the net return: the expected return on the asset, and the cost or benefit of any exchange rate movement. In the short-run, unlike the currency flows related to the trade of goods and services, hot money capital flows can reverse quickly and often.

As is the case with most things whose value is determined by human beings, foreign exchange rates very often overshoot the longer-term equilibrium level implied by fundamental variables. This is explained by the human tendency for excessive exuberance at market highs, and excessive fear at market lows. A review of the movement of the U.S. Dollar exchange rate against the German Mark or the Japanese Yen from 1979 – 1991 is an excellent demonstration of the overshooting concept.

Other variables we could place under the umbrella of fundamental analysis, so called non-economic variables, also play a role in exchange rate determination. Political and psychological variables can also have an impact on exchange rate behavior. Countries that enjoy relatively stable government and societies typically enjoy the benefits of being perceived as a safe haven currency country. In difficult time's capital quickly moves to safe haven currencies for protection. Because, in foreign exchange everything is relative.

The Euro area crisis of the past several years, and the Thai currency crisis from the 1990's, are excellent examples of non-economic variables impacting FX rates and the flow of capital across borders.

On a daily basis, in the short term, technical analysis also influences FX price movements. Especially, when there is an absence of fundamental economic information.

## Technical Analysis

This is the area of analysis which can provide a nearly level playing field between the market pro's and the day trader at home. In the absence of other market moving information, technical analysis drives daily price action. Studying technical charts at a basic level to determine near term resistance and support levels is not difficult. Because it takes years to become expert in fundamental analysis, technical analysis is pushed by retail FX brokers as the basis for success for the new FX trader: the best starting point.

Technical analysis, using past price trends to forecast future price movements, is another critical part of daily short-run exchange rate movements. Using charts of past price data we can find patterns, trends, strong points and weak points. We can look at exchange rate price data over varied periods of times and against a variety of other currencies. Technical analysis provides important buy and sell signals derived from specific chart patterns. Past price data for any financial market product, and specifically foreign exchange rates, reflects the psychological mood of market participants at any given time in the past. This information helps traders determine how market participants are likely to react when the market approaches a given price level again.

There are a variety of chart methodologies, though typically today's market participants look at line charts, bar charts, or candlestick charts. Coupled with these different chart types is a variety of stochastic charting tools (studies or signals) to help confirm a given pattern, or a strong or weak point. These tools include moving averages (MA), relative strength indexes (RSI), or retracement points (Fibonacci).

Technical analysis is focused on regularly recurring patterns. That such regular patterns exist has been very successfully proven for decades by a variety of defined patterns and technical theories such as the Elliott Wave theory, and the Fibonacci trading theory. The important factor for the forecasting power in technical analysis is the degree to which the number of market participants believes in a particular pattern or price level as a buy or sell signal. The more market participants who believe in a certain price signal, the more likely it will be that the price signal turns out to be the entry or exit point of a profitable trade.

Forecasting of exchange rates is an extremely difficult task. Opposing fundamental trends often coincide with each other, correlations exist and then disappear, and expectations of market participants vary. Technical chart points work sometimes, and sometimes they don't. Large unexpected flows of capital can lay the best strategies to waste. If you trade foreign exchange you will incur losses. The idea is to let your winning trades run, and cut your losing trades with discipline.

# Chapter 4

## The Foreign Exchange (FX) Market at Work

The FX market is made up of all buyers and sellers of foreign exchange. The majority of buyers and sellers are speculators and multinational corporations. Commercial banks (investment banks and brokerages) are the conduit between foreign exchange supply and demand. The main task of a bank's FX department is to provide access to the currency market for their customers. Customers include corporations of varying sizes, hedge funds, pension funds, government agencies, sovereign wealth funds, and day traders. At any given time customers may need to convert assets from one currency to another, hedge future financial transactions, or they may want to engage in outright speculation on the direction of a currency's future movement.

The daily volume on the foreign exchange market has grown dramatically since the U.S. abandoned the Bretton Woods system in the early 1970's. In the 1980's daily FX volume was counted in the hundreds of billions of dollars. By the late 1990's daily volume reached $1.3 trillion. Despite restrictions imposed by monetary authorities in a number of countries in Asia and eastern Europe as a result of repeated currency crises in the late 1990's and early 2000's, and significantly tightened regulations within the U.S. financial system after the recession of 2008 and the passage of the Dodd-Frank Wall Street Reform and Consumer Protection Act, daily FX volumes have continued to increase. By the end of 2012 volume in the foreign exchange market averaged approximately $4.75 trillion per day.

The major centers for FX are New York, London, and Tokyo. However, nearly every major city in every country has banks that participate in the foreign exchange market. Time zones over lap and dictate the level of liquidity in the market at any given time.

Foreign exchange trading is 24 hours a day, five days a week. Asia begins the week for U.S. traders on Sundays in New Zealand at approximately 3:00 PM EST. By the late afternoon in Asia, Europe begins their day. By lunch time in Europe, New York begins their day. By New York lunch Europe finishes their day. And, by the end of New York afternoons Asia picks it up again as New Zealand begins their next day. The trading week finishes for U.S. traders on Fridays at 5:00 PM EST in New York. The most liquid time of the day for the U.S. FX market participant is between 7:00 AM -12:00 PM EST.

Professional foreign exchange trading requires advanced infrastructure. Business is done by landline telephones (with many direct lines to important brokers and corporate treasury desks), electronic dealing systems, e-Commerce via the Internet, pricing engines, and algorithmic trading models running on powerful computers and servers using advanced software. Most FX departments use multiple dealing systems. The market leaders for electronic based dealing systems at the wholesale level are EBS, and Reuters.

For the retail day trader, FXCM (Forex Capital Markets) and CitiFX Pro (Citibank) are two of the best Internet trading platforms. They both offer competitive currency pricing (narrow interbank spreads with a brokerage fee, or wider spreads without a fee), technical charting packages, PnL systems, and discounted brokerage based on volume traded.

*A note for day traders:*
*All pricing on retail platforms is provided by brokers or commercial banks. Retail day traders are price takers; they are not allowed to be direct price makers.*

Just as the FX pros need the best equipment, so does the day trader at home.

## *Tools of the Trade*

The preferred tools of the trade for the day trader at the home office would include:

A quality computer with a powerful CPU
Dual monitors (or, one monitor over 22")
Printer
Scanner or fax
High speed Internet access
Land line telephone (or, a 100% reliable cell phone)
Television
Real-time news feed
Equity/fixed income/commodities price feed
Technical charting package
Profit and loss system (PnL)
Calculator
Economic calendar

Most online FX brokers offer trading platforms with a charting package and a PnL system. Once a trading account is funded with initial margin, and the tools are in place, the first FX trade can be executed.

An FX trader acquires his or her skills largely through experience. An important element of this experience is close cooperation among a group of traders. From the beginning to the end of the FX trading day, almost constantly, traders are doing business at the same time. When trades are executed in a particular currency pair, the rate of that currency pair and the rates of other currency pairs can change markedly. This requires that all other traders in the group be kept informed in real-time about large trades, changes in price action, if a currency pair is moving higher or lower, technical levels that are being approached or breeched, or the release a headline or data point.

For the day trader at the home office, who doesn't have the benefit of a group of likeminded traders around them, it is necessary to keep a watchful eye on a variety of variables. The day trader will have to watch other currency pairs they are not trading, know the implied correlation coefficients among currency pairs, watch the news feed, and watch other markets (like the S&P 500). This requires keeping multiple windows open on the desk top, and being able to react quickly to fast changing information.

Not good trading skills, nor advanced knowledge of macroeconomics and monetary policy, nor the best trading and communication systems are sufficient to guarantee success as an FX day trader. A high risk tolerance embedded in individual personality, quick reflexes, the ability to remain calm in the face of financial loss, and a gamblers mentality will help.

It is often said financial market speculation is nothing more than legalized gambling. OK, but you better be well informed. An understanding of economics, international economics, geo-politics, and monetary and fiscal policy can provide an advantage when it comes to trading FX.

Before learning about the FX spot market, familiarity with currency codes will help. Read through the following table.

| Currency Code | Currency | Currency Code | Currency |
|---|---|---|---|
| USD | U.S. Dollar | SEK | Swedish Krona |
| EUR | Euro | DKK | Danish Krone |
| JPY | Japanese Yen | NOK | Norwegian Krone |
| GBP | British Pound | PLN | Polish Zloty |
| CHF | Swiss Franc | CZK | Czech Koruna |
| CAD | Canadian Dollar | SGD | Singapore Dollar |
| AUD | Australian Dollar | HKD | Hong Kong Dollar |
| NZD | N. Zealand Dollar | HUF | Hungarian Forint |
| MXN | Mexican Peso | ILS | Israeli Shekel |
| RUB | Russian Ruble | TRY | Turkish Lira |
| ZAR | S. African Rand | | |

## *Spot*

Foreign exchange trades typically are for spot, or a forward date. These are known as value dates.

A spot trade is essentially a cash foreign exchange trade. The value date (date at which the transaction is settled between counterparties) is the second working day after the date on which the trade is done (this allows for the administrative handling of the deals). Since banks are closed on Saturdays and Sundays, spot trades executed on Thursdays or Fridays settle on Monday or Tuesday respectively. Spot transactions are the most common form of trade in FX.

*Spot Quotes*

For the U.S. FX trader, most spot FX quotes, prices, are stated in foreign currency terms. There are some exceptions, where the quote is in U.S. Dollar terms, most notably the British Pound (GBP), the Euro (EUR), and the Australian dollar (AUD).

The U.S. Dollar Japanese Yen exchange rate (USD/JPY) is quoted as the number of Yen per U.S. Dollar. Using the sample rate for USD/JPY of 93.75, this number would read: ninety-three point seven-five Yen per U.S. Dollar. Or, conversely, the Euro U.S. Dollar exchange rate (EUR/USD) is quoted as the number of U.S. Dollars per Euro. A sample rate for EUR/USD of 1.3250 would read: one dollar and thirty-two point five cents per Euro.

Note in the EUR/USD example the quote goes out to the 4th decimal place. As you can see below most currency pairs are publically quoted out to four decimal places. There are exceptions like USD/JPY, or cross rates like EUR/JPY that only go out two decimal places. However, when it comes to actually trading FX on electronic and Internet dealing platforms today, prices are actually quoted to the 5th decimal, or the 3[rd,] in the case of USD/JPY.

On February 22, 2013, closing rates were as indicated in the following table.

| Currency | Buying Rate (bid) | Selling Rate (offer) |
|---|---|---|
| EUR/USD | 1.3167 | 1.3171 |
| USD/JPY | 93.28 | 93.32 |
| GBP/USD | 1.5266 | 1.5270 |
| USD/CAD | 1.0238 | 1.0242 |
| USD/CHF | .9312 | .9316 |

The above buying and selling rates are applied to dealings between banks, banks and their customers, and day traders on retail platforms. Note: interbank spreads between the buying and selling rate are typically narrower then spreads on retail platforms.

If we have a quote of 93.28/93.32 for USD/JPY, the first rate is the buying rate for the U.S. Dollar and the selling rate for the Japanese Yen. The second rate is the selling rate for the U.S. Dollar and the buying rate for the Japanese Yen. Conversely, for the EUR/USD quote of 1.3167/1.3171, the first rate is the buying rate for the Euro and the selling rate for the U.S. Dollar. The second is the selling rate for the Euro and the buying rate for the U.S. Dollar.

*Remember: this is foreign exchange – exchanging one currency for another.*

Spot trades in cross currency pairs, non-U.S. Dollar currency pairs, are a big part of the total daily volume traded on FX market. Not surprisingly, banks, corporations, and investors often wish to do business against currencies other than the U.S. Dollar: for instance Euro against the Swiss Franc (CHF), or British Pound (GBP) against the JPY. In such cases we have to work out the cross rates. Cross rates are derived from the U.S. Dollar currency rates. Based on the rates above, we can determine the market cross rates for EUR/JPY, or EUR/CHF.

For purposes of this example, use the midpoint of the quoted rates above.

To calculate a EUR/JPY rate, multiply EUR/USD by USD/JPY: 1.3169 x 93.30. EUR/JPY equals 122.87. A two-way price would be 122.85 - 122.89.

To calculate a CHF/JPY rate, divide USD/JPY by USD/CHF: 93.30 ÷ .9314. CHF/JPY equals 100.17. A two-way price would be 100.14 – 100.18.

There are dozens of currency pairs to choose from for the day trader at home. Currency pairs are generally classified in groups. There are the majors, the crosses, and emerging markets. Below is a partial list of examples of each classification.

| Majors | Crosses | Emerging Markets |
|---|---|---|
| EUR/USD | EUR/JPY | USD/MXN |
| USD/JPY | EUR/GBP | USD/PLN |
| GBP/USD | EUR/CHF | USD/CZK |
| USD/CAD | GBP/JPY | USD/ZAR |
| USD/CHF | AUD/JPY | USD/TRY |
| AUD/USD | CHF/JPY | USD/RUB |

### *Forwards*

A forward FX transaction has a value date beyond the spot date and is an agreement to exchange currencies at some future date. The forward exchange price is either higher (premium) or lower (discount) than the spot price on the day the forward deal was booked. The interest rate differential between the two currencies involved in the transaction determines if the forward rate is a premium or a discount.

There are two types of forward contracts. First, an outright forward contract involves a single forward transaction. Second, a forward swap contract, which includes the money market (short-term deposits), and is composed of a simultaneous spot purchase with a forward sale (or vice versa). Forward contracts are used as a hedge against future exchange rate risk, as part of currency swaps, or to speculate on future exchange rate movements.

Forward currency rates are not quoted like spot rates. Typically only the difference in decimal points between the spot and forward prices (the premiums and discounts) are quoted. This is because forward rates don't change nearly as often as spot rates, and simple market convention has established only quoting the point's differential.

The following table is an example of how spot and forward rates are quoted and published. The rates shown are again those of February 22, 2013.

| Period | EUR/USD (bid rate) | USD/JPY (offer rate) |
|---|---|---|
| Spot price | 1.3127 – 1.3131 | 93.28 – 93.32 |
| 1 month | 2.53 – 2.74 | 20 – 19 |
| 3 months | 8.2 – 8.68 | 62 – 59.5 |
| 6 months | 16.79 – 17.92 | 147 – 132 |
| 12 months | 36.96 – 40.72 | 378 – 358 |

The forward rate is determined by either adding the premium to, or subtracting the discount from the spot rate. Forward rates do not always carry plus or minus signs: the experienced FX market participant will know from the price quoted and interest rates differentials between the two currency countries to add or subtract. The determination is easy: the bid rate is less than the offer rate.

As an example, we can figure out the 3 month forward rate for EUR/USD from the above prices:

| | EUR/USD |
|---|---|
| Spot Rate | 1.3127 – 1.3131 |
| 3 month forward rate | 8.2 – 8.68 |
| Forward Spot Rate | 1.31352 – 1.31396 |

(Note the spread widens from spot to forward)

International trade and capital flows, coupled with risk aversion to exchange rate volatility provided the need for forward operations.

Foreign exchange risk from capital flows related to assets purchases overseas can be managed by selling a currency forward. Conversely, liabilities overseas can be managed by buying a currency forward.

While in normal period's daily FX forward rates are typically stable and little changed, there are times when forward rates and currencies come under sudden and unexpected pressure.

Remembering that forward rates are a function of differing interest rates between currencies, sudden and unexpected events related to politics, economics, war, or natural disaster can cause unusual volatility in interest rates, and therefore also forward FX rates. In these situations forward rates will change relatively rapidly and rates will tend to widen sharply. The premiums or discounts for one currency against another will be affected by both the interest rate differential, and by the market's expectations about future movement in the spot rates.

While spot and forward transactions dominate daily FX market volume, currency futures and options are also widely used for hedging and market speculation.

### *Futures*

Futures contracts are another foreign exchange hedging or speculation product. They are very much like a forward contract in terms of exchanging currency at some date beyond the spot date. However, unlike forward contracts which are traded among banks and customers of banks, FX future contracts are traded on an exchange: the Chicago Mercantile Exchange (CME) in Chicago, or their 24 hour electronic dealing platform, Globex.

Because future contracts are traded on an exchange they are standardized in terms of quantities (lot size), settlement dates (3mth, 6mth, 1yr), and how they are quoted (like a spot rate but always in U.S. Dollar terms). The quarterly months on the calendar have codes; H for

March, M for June, U for September, and Z for December. The following table is an example of a typical futures quote page.

| Futures Contract | Quote |
|------------------|-------|
| EM13 (EUR/USD June 2013) | 1.3084 |
| JM13 (USD/JPY June 2013) | 1.0413 |
| AM13 (AUD/USD June 2013) | 1.0308 |
| BM13 (GBP/USD June 2013) | 1.5079 |
| CM13 (USD/CAD June 2013) | .9759 |
| SM13 (USD/CHF June 2013) | 1.0569 |

*Options*

The market for foreign exchange option contracts came about in the early 1980's. The development of options was yet another important step in helping to manage FX risks, and gave investors and corporations managing cross border currency flows another tool.

Unlike a forward transaction which locks in an obligation to exchange currency at some future date at an agreed price, the buyer or seller of an option acquires the right, though not the obligation, to exchange foreign currency at some future date at an agreed price. The option is to execute the trade, or to let the contract expire and do nothing. Options can be both a hedging instrument and a speculative instrument used to profit from exchange rate movements.

Plain vanilla options contracts are of two types:

First, there is the Call option. This gives the buyer the right to buy a certain amount of a currency at a fixed rate (strike price) at an agreed upon date in the future: the expiry date.

Second, there is the Put option. This give the buyer the right to sell a certain amount of a currency at a fixed rate (strike price) at an agreed upon date in the future: the expiry date.

The buyer of a call or a put pays a premium upfront for the right to exercise the option at some exchange rate in the future. The seller of a call or put option, the option writer, has no option and accepts the exchange risk. For this risk the seller of the option receives the premium from the buyer.

## *Price Spreads*

Decades of cross-border banking activities, international trade flows, and speculation in the FX market has come to establish standard price spreads for different currency pairs in the spot, forward, futures, and options market. The spread is the difference between the bid rate and the offer rate.

Price spreads for a given currency pair can change in a 24 hour period because of the differing levels of liquidity at any given time. Liquidity is a term used to gauge notional volume in the market that is most often directly related to the number of individual participants active in the market. During the most liquid times of the FX trading day, say New York mornings (7 AM-12 PM), spreads are at the narrowest: less than a point for the majors. During less liquid times of the FX trading day, say New York afternoons and evenings (3:30 PM-8:00 PM), spreads are at their widest: 3-5 points for the majors.

For the day trader using one of the handful of the most popular Internet based FX brokerage platforms, the spread and brokerage fees are closely connected and an important part of marketing strategy. Brokerage platforms that offer the narrow interbank spreads, less than a point in the majors, or two to three points in the crosses, charge a per trade brokerage fee. Other platforms that emphasize that they don't charge a brokerage fee make their money by offering a wider spread, like 3-5 points in the majors, or 5-7 points in the crosses. Since these brokerage platforms still have access to the tight interbank spreads behind the scenes at their home trading floor, they can in theory earn at least 2-5 points per trade; essentially a broker's fee.

For the day trader with a longer-term view, no brokerage fee and the wider spread may work since giving up 2-4 points on entry will have little bearing on a profitable strategy. For the more active short-term day trader, the narrower spread with a fee may work since giving up 2-4 points per trade may be more expensive.

## *Buy & Sell | Long & Short*

From a behind the scenes accounting perspective, commercial banks maintain accounts in most currencies for the purpose of managing the cash flows of their FX activity. These accounts are called nostro accounts: a bank account held in a foreign country by a domestic bank, denominated in the currency of that country. Like any account maintained with any bank, nostro accounts can't be overdrawn for long if at all, and are therefore maintained daily to ensure proper balances.

In FX, a long position results in credit balances in a nostro account (buying EUR selling USD), and a short position (selling EUR buying USD) results in debit balances in a nostro account. If we buy the Euro against the U.S. Dollar we will be long Euros and short U.S. Dollars. If we sell the Euro against the U.S. Dollar we will be short Euros and long U.S. Dollars. Holding a currency spot position overnight (beyond the spot date) will require rolling over the position to the next spot date using forwards - swaps, to ensure the nostro account for the short currency is properly funded.

Changes in FX positions occur throughout the day.  Traders in big banks have to know their net position at all times.  If we start the day with a long EUR/USD position of €7,000,000, and later sell €2,000,000 and then sometime later €3,000,000 more, our long position is reduced to €2,000,000.  Thankfully, for day traders most online FX brokerage platforms include real-time PnL systems that keep up to date on position size, and profits or losses. (SBC, 1992)

Position sizes, or trade amounts, for the day trader using a retail platform in the home office are not in the millions of the base currency, but rather they are in lots.  Lots are usually traded in 10's, and one lot relates to one thousand of the base currency.

For instance:

Buying 1000 lots in EUR/USD at a price of 1.3171 means buying €1,000,000 and selling $1,317,100 (€1,000,000 X 1.3171)

Using advanced software programs, a bank's FX department keeps constant track of their long/short positions in various currencies, and their associated risk based on real time revaluations.  Since many counter-parties trade with each other more than once per day in different currencies and amounts, administrative netting of long/short positions helps in the clearing of foreign exchange transactions.  In the face of increasing daily volume, netting has markedly helped keep clearing costs down.

From the perspective of the trader in a bank or the day trader at home, to be long or short relates to the simple act of buying or selling. There are different phrases for these actions.  For traders it involves bidding or offering, buying or selling, or declaring the words give or take, or yours or mine.

Bidding, buying, taking, and mine are actions and words used to get long in the FX market.  Bidding (wait to buy) involves entering a price in the market and waiting for a seller to deal on your price.  Buying, taking, and mine all involve getting into a long FX position (or exiting a short position) by dealing on the offered price in the market.

Offering, selling, giving, and yours are actions and words used to get short in the FX market.  Offering (wait to sell) involves entering a price in the market and waiting for a buyer to deal on your price.  Selling, giving, and yours all involve getting into a short FX position (or exiting a long position) by dealing on the bid price in the market.

Regardless of the asset class, we've all heard the phrase: buy low and sell high.  In FX trading there is also: sell high and buy low.  Unlike the stock market getting short in FX is as easy as getting long.  While the basic concept is the same for all asset classes, in FX a trader can be thought of as being long and short at the same time.

Remember, this is foreign *exchange*.  A long position in a currency pair, say EUR/USD, means buying EUR and selling USD: so long EUR, short USD.  A short position in EUR/USD means selling EUR and buying USD: so short EUR, long USD.  If we have long and short positions in more than one currency pair, it's important to use the U.S. Dollar as the common denominator.  Since most currency pairs are quoted in terms of dollars it is not hard to do.  However, in the case of the EUR or the GBP, simple multiplication is all that is required to find the U.S. Dollar amount.

## *Market Orders*

Managing risk in the FX market is a critical component of success.  From the FX desk of the biggest commercial bank in the world, to the day trader at home limit orders are a key element of daily risk management.  Limit orders are used to minimize financial risk, and are widely utilized in the foreign exchange market. Limit orders are typically used to take profit on a winning trade, or stop out a losing trade.

A trader should make use of a limit order when they are unable to manage a position directly because they are away from the desk, or a position is held overnight while asleep, or even if they just don't trust their own discipline. Limit orders instruct a third party how to manage your open FX position.

There are take profit (T/P) orders, and there are stop loss (S/L) orders. The exchange rate of a T/P order for a long position is above the prevailing spot price, or for a short position below the prevailing spot price. The exchange rate of a S/L order for a long position is below the prevailing spot price, or for a short position above the prevailing spot price.

For example, let's say you're long $100,000 USD/JPY (10 lots) at a rate of 93.30. Mid-day arrives and you must attend a lunch meeting. You like the long position and don't want to square up before going to lunch. So, you leave a limit order with your broker. Your S/L level is 93.10, and your T/P level is 93.70. This is how to write/enter the order:

Sell $100,000 USD/JPY at 93.10 S/L, or 93.70 T/P, OCO

OCO stands for one-cancels-the-other. If the T/P rate is executed the S/L side of the order is cancelled.

Limit orders can also be used to enter a position. Here to, they are used when a trader is unable to be at the trading desk, or during overnight hours. Using the USD/JPY rate above, if the market is presently trading at 93.30, and it is predicted the exchange rate will go lower and accelerate through support at 93.10 towards 92.50, a S/L order can be used to get short at or near 93.10. An order is left with a broker to get short USD/JPY, and an order to manage the risk if the first order is done is also established: an "if done" order.

It would read like this:

Sell $100,000 USD/JPY at 93.10 S/L
*If done*
Buy $100,000 USD/JPY at 93.30 S/L, or 92.50 T/P

So, if the market goes lower as predicted the first order to get short USD/JPY at 93.10 will get executed. The second order will then be in force to manage the newly opened FX position.

   S/L orders are executed at the next best price after the S/L price trades. Depending on the volatility of the market around an S/L rate, orders are rarely executed at the stated price. The so called slippage can be 1 pip, or it could be a whole spread 3-pips or more. Specific instructions can be conveyed to the third party managing the order to attempt to reduce slippage, though there is no guarantee the S/L rate upon execution will match the order rate. For T/P orders, more often than not they are executed at the stated exchange rate. It is much easier to sell in a market going higher then to sell in a market going lower.

   A trailing stop can also be used. A trailing stop instructs a third party to raise or lower (depending on the position) the stop loss rate. A trailing stop is a method to give back less money in the swings of market price action as a trade approaches or is in profitability

*A good rule is: let your winners run, and cut your losers. Be disciplined.*

## *Daily Preparation*

Each morning, at banks, hedge funds, and brokerages around the world the chief dealers and traders of the foreign exchange department will hold a morning meeting. At these meetings traders discuss overnight activity, fundamental economic indicators, central bank activities, technical price levels, strategy, and take note of other related market headlines that will help guide their outlook for the day's trading ahead.

With the morning meeting complete, market participants are prepared for the start of business. Big banks and the like don't just carry out the orders of their customers; they trade on their own accounts. They use the banks money to make more money for the bank.

The day trader at home should engage in a morning meeting of their own. If possible, try to include other day traders via conference call. Scheduling an hour before the start of trading should provide enough time to review overnight headlines (Asia, the Middle East, and Europe), review technical charts to analyze the overnight price action and to determine support and resistance points, take note of posted highs and lows of relevant currency pairs, check other financial markets, look at the day's economic calendar, and plan the day's strategy.

On days without economic data releases, a quiet news wire, or no meaningful size capital flows through the market, technical trading will dominate. The day trader must allow enough time to study the charts each day before trading. Not just the charts of the currency pair to be traded, but also the charts of other major currency pairs because of the important information found in the implied correlations in FX.

## *Retail FX*

In 2013, the playing field for professional FX traders in a bank vs. the day traders at home has never been so level in terms of market access, spreads, and technical analysis. Even functionality, while still not ideal for the retail FX trader, the gap is narrow.

There are important areas where retail FX is still disadvantaged:

Utilizing pricing engines Internet FX brokers are beholden to banks for market pricing. During fast moving markets FX desks at commercial banks become busy and their ability to manage pricing, market orders, and limit orders is compromised. During fast moving markets retail FX traders give up some profitability due to poor execution and slow trade confirmation.

Retail traders give up execution speed by not having the use of key pads that the pros use. Retail traders are limited to the mouse, and key strokes on the keyboard for entering prices and market orders.

Retail traders are not allowed to be price makers with the ability to narrow the spread by bidding or offering inside the market price, or the ability to join the bid or offer as a market maker.

Retail traders give up real-time information on corporate and speculative money flows.

Even so, retail FX brokers offer the day trader a tremendous opportunity to trade the biggest, most liquid, least regulated market in the world. The FX market offers unique portfolio diversification, above average annual returns, and for those willing to put in the time, potentially a very good living.

The number of retail players in the space is growing monthly. As employment for professional FX traders at commercial banks continues to get squeezed by algorithmic trading models, pricing engines and the roll out of the Volker Rule from the Dodd-Frank Wall Street Reform and Consumer Protection Act, retail FX is expanding.

The big names in Internet FX brokerage are FXCM, CitiFX Pro, Onada, Saxo, and TDAmeritrade just to name a handful. There are dozens of options to choose from, and there is now a growing retail boutique style FX voice brokerage model developing offering capital access and third party execution.

Margin and leverage are what makes the FX market accessible to the day trader at home. Thanks to leverage ratios of 50:1, with a few thousand dollars a trader can put on trade sizes in the hundreds of thousands. With $25,000, a day trader can trade millions. Margin is the pool of money from which losses are taken, and margin amounts combined with leverage ratios dictate notional position size.

# Chapter 5

# FX Risk Management

We can categorize foreign exchange risk in four ways: financial risk, transaction risk, systems risk, and credit risk. None of these risk types can be successfully managed individually, and each requires different measures to manage properly (SBC, 1992).

### *Financial Risk*

Financial risk refers to losses from foreign exchange transactions, be it in the spot, forward, futures, or options market.

Financial risk comes from open positions, un-hedged positions, in the FX market. It begins the moment a trade is executed, and can be minimized by the use of trading limits.

In the spot market, risk can be minimized by the use of limits: intraday trading limits for traders (maximum daily loss allowed), daily position limits (maximum position size), and overnight trading limits which incorporates both trading and position limits for overnight markets.

In the forward and futures markets, limits again help control risk. A forward position is exposed to both exchange rate and interest rate fluctuations. Limits are imposed on losses, positions size, and the maturity date. The shorter the maturity date, the less is the interest rate risk. Another way to minimize risk in the forward market is to manage the forward book to maximize matched maturities (duration).

Financial risk in the options market involves many of the same use of limits as the spot and forward/futures markets. With options though, we add time decay. There is an inverse relationship between the options price and the decrease in time to expiration. As the agreed upon option expiry date approaches the value of the option is reduced because the probability of the option being profitable (in-the-money) drops. With an in-the-money option time decay can work more rapidly. Of course, the risk to the buyer of an option contract is just the premium paid. The seller however has considerably more risk since they are exposed to exchange rate movements.

For the day trader at home financial risk is number one on the list. Self imposed limits must be adhered to. Most importantly, position limits and stop/loss limits must be set. Trading on margin and using leverage allows for larger position sizes than any given amount of capital would otherwise allow. With that comes greater risk. We can trade with leverage because the trade size amounts are notional, used only to calculate payments: profits and losses. What matters is the net gain (loss) of each trade, and assuming asset prices don't quickly go to zero, margin accounts only need cover daily losses. Larger position sizes require more margin because the potential for loss is greater, and can arise more quickly.

### Transaction Risk

Transaction risk involves the daily conduct of foreign exchange activities from the initial execution of the trade, to confirmation of the trade, to proper cash flow payments and settlement.

From an individual or employee perspective, it is about performance. Personality must align with the nature and stress of the fast-paced high-pressure world of the foreign exchange market. Educational initiatives must be maintained to manage ongoing technological and methodological changes. Discipline in adhering to set limits must be maintained at all times. Trade tickets and confirmations must be free of typos and clerical errors. Fat finger trades must not occur. For the trader at a commercial bank transaction risk is about execution and deal confirmation. For the day trader at home, transaction risk is primarily about execution. This is the fat finger trade: the out trade. The day trader at home must be careful to trade the correct amount, trade in the correct window pane, know if long or short and by how much, put in correct price levels on orders, remember orders left in the market, and generally pay close attention to their activities.

### Systems Risk

Systems risk refers to the dealing platform used, the communications system, the trade reporting system, the front-end profit and loss system, and the payments system. Quality system management is one of the best ways to reduce risk when participating in the foreign exchange market. You can have the best people with the best ideas and tremendous risk management: it would all be for nothing if the systems eliminate profits. Poor system functionality, latency issues related to deal execution and confirmation, and the untimely exchange of payments can ruin the best FX strategies.

An FX participant must have access to the best pricing, an excellent PnL and position management system, an automatic and efficient trade confirmation system, and a back office that ensures the timely transfer of payments on a net basis.

For the day trader, systems risk relates to the quality of the brokerage dealing platform that is selected. How does the system perform during a fast moving market? How quickly are trades confirmed? Are orders executed in a timely manner and within a spread of your indicated price? In the event of a screen freeze or an out trade will your call to the trade team be answered quickly?

### *Credit Risk*

Credit risk primarily relates to counter-parties (other banks or corporate customers) who may not live up to the payment obligations they entered into when a foreign exchange transaction was concluded. Banks use trading limits on counter-parties based on credit evaluations. Margin requirements are imposed, and often collateral is asked to be set aside before FX transactions can begin. Credit risk involves consideration of settlement risk, or country risk based on politics, war, and natural disaster.

For the day trader, counter-party credit risk is about the financial health and integrity of the FX broker selected with which to open a margin account. Will the profits earned from trading be there to transfer back to a personal account? Will margin capital be there when the account is closed? Is the selected broker taking open positions in the market and risking client margin capital? Additionally, the day trader must consider and monitor the financial health of the bank the selected broker uses to park client funds.

# Chapter 6

## How to Trade FX

There is more than one way to profitably trade the FX market. Buy low sell high works. Sell high buy low also works. Ideally each FX trader develops their own system: a tried and true method of making money that can be replicated. Developing a trading system takes time, and until that time trial and error is as always the starting point. As was discussed in Chapter 3, technical analysis is the refuge of the rookie FX trader. Many traders have a system solely dependent on technical analysis, ignoring fundamental indicators, breaking news events, or unusual capital flows.

You can trade the data, you can trade the charts, you can trade central bank meetings and policy announcements, you can trade headlines, you can trade off of correlations, or you can focus on arbitrage opportunities. Either way, you're winning trades have to earn more than your losing trades lose. Let the winners run and cut those losers.

Start with these simple steps:

### Step 1

Open an FX brokerage account. There are options as to the type. There are full service online retail FX brokers that charge a brokerage fee, some that don't, and some that offer a choice. There are also FX brokers who let day trader's trade off of their capital requiring a smaller initial margin for the day trader. And, there are voice brokers who work over the phone, provide capital to trade with, provide quotes and price action updates, FX advisory, execute trades, and manage risk on behalf of clients.

The basics needed from a full service FX broker include narrow and consistent price spreads, a Pnl reporting system, technical charting, a quick and easy method of price entry and trade execution, workspace personalization, timely confirmation of trades, and limited fund transfer constraints. There are many retail online FX brokers who offer demo accounts for practice.

### Step 2

Fund the brokerage account with initial margin. The greater the initial margin, the larger the position size (depending on the leverage offered by the selected FX broker).

**Warning: more margin, more leverage - greater risk.**

Assuming 50:1 leverage, a day trader using a full service online retail FX broker should have initial margin of at least $1,000. For a voice broker providing access to their capital, initial margin should be at least $250. A $1,000 margin account using current rates would allow for a maximum position size in say, EUR/USD, of 30 lots (€30,000, or $39,300 using a spot rate of 1.3100). A ten PIP profit on a 30 lot EUR/USD position would equal $30.00.

### Step 3

Read this book again. And, spend a at least a few days watching the FX majors and some crosses trade to get familiar with the price action, correlations, and how different currency pairs react to market news.

### Step 4

Choose a currency pair to trade and identify those pairs to monitor because of close correlations to the pair traded. EUR/USD, USD/JPY, EUR/JPY, GBP/USD, USD/CAD, AUD/USD are some of the most liquid currency pairs in the FX market. Emerging market currencies are typically the least liquid. It is a good idea for a rookie to begin with a more liquid currency pair.

### Step 5

Pick a start date and time that coincides with one of the 25 U.S. economic indicators listed in Chapter 8.

### Step 6

Prepare for trading day ahead. Formulate a view on the market based on fundamental and technical information analyzed during morning prep.

### Step 7

Execute and confirm an FX trade with a mouse, button clicks, or a phone call motivated by a fundamental indicator, technical indicator, or unique price action related to a headline news event.

### Step 8

Manage the position. Quickly establish a stop loss limit rate based on prudent risk/reward analysis that allows for per trade profits to be greater than per trade losses. Risking 20 pips to earn 5 pips is not a risk/reward scenario that will allow for a margin account to stay well funded for long. Determining a stop loss and take profit level will depend on market volatility, each trader's individually determined risk tolerance, the time element, and/or the desired profitability of the trade.

This is the part where discipline is required. Traders who do not adhere to financially determined stop loss limits will wipe out their margin accounts quickly.  Those who don't adhere to take profit levels can see those profits taken right back in a quick reversal.

When placing limit orders, often times a trailing stop is utilized.  As a position moves towards profitability, or once a position is in the money, a trailing stop instructs a third party to raise or lower (depending on the position) the stop loss rate.

### Step 9

Exit position.  After careful monitoring, exit position at S/L or T/P level using a mouse, button clicks, or a phone call.

### Step 10

Confirm proper position and PnL accounting based on number of pips earned or lost.

### Step 11

Repeat, and repeat, and repeat.

# Chapter 7

## Language of the Foreign Exchange (FX) Market

This chapter is not a glossary. It is important for an FX trader to know the lingo of the business. The day trader at the home office is not exposed to the critical mass of people all doing the same thing on the trading floor of a commercial bank. In order to shorten the learning curve it is important for the day trader at home to study the words and phrases in this chapter.

*Learn it, Know it, Use it*

**Algo**
Short hand used for algorithmic trading model. A financial market model using algorithms to replicate human trading behavior in the digital world. At the time of this writing Algo's have come to dominate the FX market since their introduction in late 2005.

**Arbitrage**
The near simultaneous purchase and sale of an asset in order to profit from a difference in the price within the market or on different platforms. Arbitrage results from market inefficiencies.

**Balance of Payments (BOP)**
An accounting of all transactions between a country and the rest of the world. BOP is the sum of the current account and capital account and should equal zero.

**Bank of Mexico**
The central bank of Mexico.

**BIS**
Bank of International Settlements. The central bank of central banks located in Basel, Switzerland.

**BOC**
Bank of Canada. The central bank of Canada.

**BOJ**
Bank of Japan. The central bank of Japan.

**Break-even point**
In options, the market price that the underlying asset must reach for option buyers to avoid a loss if they exercise. In the case of a call option, the break-even point is the exercise price plus the premium, and in the case of a put option, the exercise price minus the premium.

**Bretton-Woods System**
System of fixed exchange rates based on the price of gold in terms of U.S. Dollars established at the end of WWII during a conference in Bretton-Woods, New Hampshire hosted by the U.S. & Britain.

**Buying|Bid rate**
The left side of a two-way price quote: the rate at which the price maker is willing to buy FX.

**Call option**
This gives the buyer the right, but not the obligation to buy a certain amount of a currency at a fixed rate (strike price) at an agreed upon date in the future: the expiry date.

**Capital account**
One of two components of a nation's balance of payments, it is a measure of a country's net export position of financial capital including the central bank's foreign exchange reserves.

## Central bank
The institution responsible for overseeing the monetary system of a nation, or group of nations. They supervise the banking system, set short-term interest rates, maintain price stability, and in some cases, foster growth.

## Composite index
A standardized grouping of indexes or asset prices providing a statistical measure.

## Cross rate
Exchange rates that do not include the U.S. Dollar (USD).

## Currency
A generally accepted form of money (means of exchange), including coins and paper notes, which is issued by a government and circulated within an economy.

## Currency basket
A selected group of currencies in which the weighted average is used as a measure of the value or the amount of an obligation.

## Current account
A measure of county's net export position of goods and services plus net foreign earnings.

## Delta
The ratio comparing the change in the price of the underlying asset to the corresponding change in the price of an option. Sometimes referred to as the hedge ratio.

## Delta hedging
An action required by FX options traders in order to keep the proper hedge on for a given option position which involves the buying or selling in the spot market in relation to the change in price of the currency.

## Devaluation
A fall in the external value of a currency in a freely floating exchange rate system.

## Diffusion Index
A measure of the degree to which components of an index have changed from month-to-month: no change, increase, or decrease.

## Dirty float
A system of floating exchange rates characterized by regular central bank interventions to influence the exchange rate.

## Discount
When the forward market rate is lower than the spot rate today. Forward discounts are subtracted from the current spot rate.

## Dodd|Frank
Dodd |Frank Wall Street Reform and Consumer Protection Act. A regulatory law passed by the U.S. Congress in 2010 in response to the housing and banking crisis that brought about the great recession of 2008.

## Duration
The time until principle repayment of a fixed income instrument is due.

## ECB
European Central Bank. The central bank for the Euro area, a 17-member European currency block.

**ETF**
Exchange Traded Fund. An index fund with a basket of assets that trades like a stock.

**Eurodollar (fixed income)**
U.S. Dollar deposits in British, or Euro zone country banks.

**Exchange controls**
Restrictions put in place by national governments meant to control the flow of foreign exchange across borders associated with trade and financial transactions.

**Exchange rate**
The price of one currency in terms of another.

**Exercise price**
Strike price of an option.

**Expiry day**
The last day on which an option can be exercised.

**External value**
Purchasing power of one currency vs. another currency.

**Fed**
Federal Reserve Bank of the United States. The central bank of the U.S.

**Fiscal policy**
The process of allocating and managing government revenues and expenditures. Policy carried out by the legislative or executive branch of government for the purpose of impacting macroeconomic conditions using tax rates and expenditure levels.

### Fixed exchange rate
A government set exchange rate for a nation's currency in relation to the price of another asset like gold or another currency, requiring daily manipulation in both the FX market and the domestic money market.

### Floating
Open and free determination of market exchange rates.

### FOMC
Federal Open Market Committee.  Group within the U.S. Fed that sets monetary policy.

### Forwards
Foreign exchange transactions that are agreed to take place at some date in the future beyond two days (spot settlement).

### Futures
Standardized foreign exchange transactions that take place at fixed dates in the future beyond two days (spot settlement) and are traded on an exchange (CME, GLOBEX).

### Hedge Fund
Private investment funds typically known for being more active in gaining returns and engaging in greater risk.

### Hedging
A risk management tool used to offset open positions to secure against losses due to price fluctuations.

### HMA
Hong Kong Monetary Authority.  Hong Kong governing authority responsible for maintaining monetary stability.

## IMF
International Monetary Fund, established in 1944 at the Bretton Woods Conference.

## Inflation
The rate of change of prices in an economy over a given period of time as measured by an index like the Consumer Price Index (CPI).

## Initial margin
The amount deposited in a brokerage account necessary to begin trading.

## Intervention
Central bank participation in the currency market in order to strengthen or weaken their domestic currency.

## In-the-money
For a call option, when the option's strike price is below the market price of the underlying asset.
For a put option, when the strike price is above the market price of the underlying asset.

## Leverage
Using borrowed capital to increase returns. Used in coordination with margin accounts.

## LIBOR
London Interbank Offered rate. A series of short-term interest rates set by a group of commercial banks and used as a basis for lending.

## Liquidity
A reference to the number of market participants, and therefore the volume of capital at work, in a market at a given time.

## Lot size
The standardized quantity used by retail FX brokers indicating the notional amount of the currency traded.  Usually expressed in 10's.

## Margin account
Money in a broker account that allows an investor to borrow capital.  Usually used with leverage, it is a pool of money from which financial losses on notional amounts are taken.

## Monetary policy
Central bank process of determining the size of a nation's money supply focused on short-term interest rates utilizing open market operations.

## Money market
Fixed income market with very short maturities used as a place to park large pools of capital, access short term corporate funding needs, and is considered a safe haven during volatile times.

## Money supply (U.S.)
M1: sum of currency outstanding and balances held in checking accounts.
M2: M1 plus savings deposits, time deposits, and money market mutual funds.

## MPC
Monetary Policy Committee.  The group responsible for monetary policy at the Bank of England.

## Mutual Fund
A pool of money from many investors to purchase financial assets to gain a return.

## Nostro account
A bank account held in a foreign country by a domestic bank, denominated in the currency of that country. Nostro accounts are used to facilitate settlement of foreign exchange and merchandise trade transactions.

## OCO
One cancels the other. Used when placing FX orders including both a stop loss level and a take profit level. If the top profit level is reached, the position is exited and so the stop loss limit is no longer needed.

## O/N
Overnight. Value date one day less than spot settlement.

## OPEC
Organization of Petroleum Exporting Countries. There are 12 countries: Algeria, Angola, Ecuador, Iran, Kuwait, Libya, Nigeria, Qatar, Saudi Arabia, United Arab Emirates, and Venezuela.

## Open market operations
Daily central bank activity in concert with the commercial banking system used to manage a country's money supply.

## OTC trading
Over-the-counter: financial products traded outside of an exchange.

## Out-of-the-money
For a call option, when the option's strike price is above the market price of the underlying asset.
For a put option, when the option's strike price is below the market price of the underlying asset.

**Outright forward**
A speculative purchase or sale of a forward contract as a bet on the costs to carry a currency position forward.

**PBOC**
People's Bank of China. The central bank of China.

**Pips**
In the FX market they are the last decimal place in a price quote and are tallied by traders as a measure of profit or loss.

**PnL**
Profit and Loss. Measures daily success or failure of trading decisions. A day trader's daily income statement.

**Premium**
When the forward market rate is higher than the spot rate today. Forward premiums are added to the current spot rate.

**Put option**
This gives the buyer the right, though not the obligation to sell a certain amount of a currency at a fixed rate (strike price) at an agreed upon date in the future: the expiry date.

**QE**
Quantitative easing: Unusual and outsized open market operations by a central bank implemented when short term interest rates are at their lower bound and full employment and or price stability have not yet been established.

**Quotes**
A real-time price of a currency pair. Quotes can be two-way: both the bid and ask. Or, quotes can be one-way: the bid or the offer.

**RBA**
Reserve Bank of Australia.  The central bank of Australia.

**Revaluation**
A rise in the external value of a currency in a freely floating exchange rate system.

**Rollover**
Extending the maturity of a foreign exchange position.

**SDR's**
Special Drawing Rights.  A reserve currency established in the late 1960's by the IMF to help member countries manage their domestic currency in the face of balance of payments imbalances.

**Selling | Bid rate**
The right side of a two-way price quote; the rate at which the price maker is willing to sell FX.

**SNB**
Swiss National Bank.  Central bank of Switzerland.

**S/N**
Spot next.  An FX transaction with a value date one day after the spot date.

**Spot market**
The cash market in FX.  Trades are settled within two business days.

**Squaring up (positions)**
Exiting an open position.

**Stop loss order (S/L)**
An FX order used to limit losses on a trade with instructions to buy or to sell a given amount of foreign exchange if the rate rises above or falls below a specific exchange rate.

**Strike price**
The fixed price at which the owner of an option can either buy or sell the underlying currency.

**Strong currency**
A currency with sustained price appreciation vs. other currencies.

**Swap transaction**
Related to forwards, a swap is the purchase or sale of one currency against another currency with a specific maturity date, and a simultaneous sale or purchase for a later maturity date.

**T/N**
Tomorrow next. A currency transaction where the spot side becomes due on the day after the day on which the transaction was done, and where the forward side becomes due on the day after the spot value date.

**T/P**
Take profit. An acronym used with FX orders to exit positions that are in the money.

**Theta**
A measure of time decay in the options market. Indicates the price change of an option over a period of time.

**Time deposits**
Funds invested in a bank for a pre-determined time and at a specific interest rate. Certificates of Deposit (CD's) are the most common.

**Trailing stop**
Instructs a third party to raise or lower (depending on the position) the stop loss rate as a position approaches or is in profitability.

**Value date**
A fixing date for an asset that fluctuates in price. The settlement date.

**Vanilla option**
A normal call or put option.

**Vega**
Measures an option's sensitivity to the volatility of the underlying asset.

**Volatility**
A measure of the variation in the price of an asset over time.

**Weak currency**
A currency with sustained price depreciation vs. other currencies.

**Yield curve**
A graphical expression of the level of interest rates from the very short-term to the long-term. The U.S. Treasury yield curve from 3 months to 30 years is one of most watched.

# Chapter 8

## U.S. Economic Indicators

Every day all over the world economic information is made available to financial market participants to gauge the health of the economy for most nations.  In the U.S., there are dozens of important economic indicators released each month that reveal the strength or weakness of the U.S. economy.  Financial market participants closely watch the release of these indicators.  FX price action in response to these data releases depends on how each indicator compares to the expectations of market participants as set by market economists who attempt to forecast each economic indicator.

When it comes to fundamental analysis for trading and investing, it begins with studying the economic indicators.

Among the many dozens of public and private economic indicators released each month, there is a core group of 25 U.S. economic indicators that must be monitored by any market participant.  These data points are released on a regular basis and are often subject to revision months after their initial release.  Some indicators are released weekly, some monthly, and others on a quarterly basis.

Below is a list of the most important indicators for the U.S. economy in the order they are released.  They are released each month, and every FX trader should pay attention to their release time and date.  Most data is released between 8:15 AM and 10:00 AM EST.  The main release times are 8:30 AM and 10:00 AM.

**Initial Unemployment Claims (IC) -** *(weekly) (thousands)*
Provided by the U.S. Department of Labor, IC are released every Thursday morning at 8:30am EST for the week ending the prior

Saturday. The number, counted in the thousands, indicates how many Americans file for unemployment benefits for the first time as a result of losing their jobs. Along with the headline number, there is also a Continuing Claims number that reveals how many Americans remain in the program and is counted in the millions.

## Institute for Supply Management Manufacturers Purchasing Managers Index (ISM-M) – *(monthly) (index)*

Provided by the Institute for Supply Management, the ISM-M is released monthly as a diffusion index. According to the ISM: "...this report shows the percentage reporting each response, the net difference between the number of responses in the positive economic direction (higher, better and slower for Supplier Deliveries) and the negative economic direction (lower, worse and faster for Supplier Deliveries), and the diffusion index." THE iSM-M gauges the relative strength of the manufacturing sector in the U.S. economy. A PMI™ reading above 50 percent indicates that the manufacturing economy is generally expanding; below 50 percent indicates that it is generally declining.

## Institute for Supply Management Non-Manufacturers Purchasing Managers Index (ISM-NM) – *(monthly) (index)*

Provided by the Institute for Supply Management, the ISM-NM is released monthly as a composite index. According to the ISM: "...survey responses reflect the change, if any, in the current month compared to the previous month. For each of the indicators measured this report shows the percentage reporting each response, and the diffusion index. The ISM-NM is a composite index based on the diffusion indexes for four of the indicators with equal weights. An index reading above 50 percent indicates that the non-manufacturing economy in that index is generally expanding; below 50 percent indicates that it is generally declining.

**Construction Spending (CS)** – *(monthly) (percent change)*
Provided by the U.S. Dept. of Commerce, Census Bureau, CS is released monthly for the period two months prior. It indicates the percent change in the dollar value of new construction activity in the public and private sectors.

**Factory Orders (FO) – (monthly) (percent change)**
Provided by the U.S. Dept. of Commerce, Census Bureau, FO is released monthly for the period two months prior. FO indicate the percent change in the dollar value of new orders for durable goods (goods that last more than five years) and non-durable goods.

**ADP Employment Report (ADP)** – *(monthly) (thousands)*
Provided by the private payroll company ADP, the employment report is released on the Wednesdays before the first Friday of each month at 8:15am EST. This number estimates the net employment growth in the private sector over the prior month. It does not include government employment.

**Employment Situation Summary** – *(monthly)*
Provided by the U.S. Dept. of Labor, the Employment report indicates the health of the U.S. labor market on a monthly basis. It is released on the first Friday of every month, and indicates net job growth, the unemployment rate, the length in hours of the average workweek, and average hourly earnings. This is the most closely watched data point in the financial and economic world.

> **Non-farm Payrolls (NFP)** *(thousands)*
> **Unemployment Rate (URATE)** *(percent)*
> **Average Work Week (AWW)** *(percent change)*
> **Average Hourly Earnings (AHE)** *(percent change)*

**International Trade Balance (TB)** – *(monthly) (billions)*
Provided by the U.S. Dept. of Commerce, Census Bureau, the TB is released monthly for the period two months prior. The TB reveals the net exports (exports minus imports) of goods and services for the U.S. economy.

**Retail Sales (RS)** – *(monthly) (percent change)*
Provided by the U.S. Dept. of Commerce, Census Bureau, RS is released monthly for the prior month. RS is a measure of total receipts at retail outlets. RS accounts for nearly half of total consumer spending and is therefore a good indicator of consumer spending trends.

**Producer Price Index (PPI)** – *(monthly) (percent change)*
Provided by the U.S. Bureau of Labor Statistics, the PPI is released monthly for the prior month. According to the BLS, the PPI is a family of indexes that measures the average change over time in the selling prices received by domestic producers of goods and services. The PPI measures price changes from the perspective of the seller.

**Consumer Price Index (CPI)** – *(monthly) (percent change)*
Provided by the U.S. Bureau of Labor Statistics, the CPI is released monthly for the prior month. According to the BLS, the CPI is a measure of the average change over time in the prices paid by urban consumers for a market basket of consumer goods and services.

**Empire State Mfg Survey (ESI)** – *(monthly) (index)*
Provided by the Federal Reserve Bank of New York, the ESI is released monthly for the current month. The headlines index (General Business Conditions Index) from the ESI is a diffusion index. According to the New York Fed: "Participants from across the state in a variety of industries respond to a questionnaire and report the change in a variety of indicators from the previous month. Respondents also state the likely direction of these same indicators six months ahead." Empire State: adopted nickname of New York State.

**Treasury International Capital Flows (TIC)** – *(monthly) (billions)*
Provided by the Dept. of Treasury, TIC measures the net appetite on the part of foreign nationals for U.S. Treasury debt, U.S. Agency Debt (Fannie Mae & Freddie Mac), and U.S. corporate debt.

**U of Michigan Consumer Sentiment Index (MCS)** – *(monthly) (index)*
Provided by the University of Michigan Institute for Social Research, the MCS measures how Americans view their financial condition and their view of the economy. This MCS is released twice per month (first and fourth weeks) for the current month. The second release is a revision of the first.

**Housing Starts (HS)** – *(monthly) (thousands of units on annualized basis)*
Provided by the U.S. Dept. of Commerce, Census Bureau, HS is released monthly for the prior month. HS measure the number of new foundations in the ground.

**Existing Homes Sales (XHS)** – *(monthly) (millions of units on annualized)*
Provided by the National Association of Realtors, XHS is released monthly for the prior month. XHS measures the number of units sold of homes that had a prior owner that is not the original builder.

**Durable Goods Orders (DG)** – *(monthly) (percent change)*
Provided by the U.S. Dept. of Commerce, Census Bureau, DG are released monthly for the prior month. DG measure new orders for domestic manufacturers of goods that typically last longer than five years.

**New Home Sales (NHS)** – *(monthly) (thousands of units on annualized)*
Provided by the U.S. Dept. of Commerce, Census Bureau, NHS are released monthly for the prior month. NHS measures the sale of newly constructed homes with a locked buyer.

**Consumer Confidence (CC)** – *(monthly) (index)*
Provided by the Conference Board (a private membership and research organization), CC is released monthly for the current month. CC is a survey that measures consumers' view on current economic conditions, and their six-month expectations.

**Pending Home Sales Index (PHS)** – *(monthly) (index)*
Provided by the National Association of Realtors, PHS is released monthly for the prior month. Considered a leading indicator for housing, PHS represents homes that are in contract but have not yet closed.

**Chicago Purchasing Managers Index (CPMI)** – *(monthly) (index)*
Provided by the Institute for Supply Management, the CPMI is released monthly for the current month. The CPMI is a diffusion index that measures business conditions in the Chicago area.

**Gross Domestic Product (GDP)** – *(monthly) (percent change)*
Provided by the U.S. Bureau of Economic Analysis (BEA), GDP is released monthly for the prior quarter. There are three releases: advance, preliminary, and final. The second release is a revision of the first, and the third release is a revision of the second. GDP measures the total value of U.S. economic output, both in nominal terms, and in real terms.

**Current Account (CA)** – *(quarterly) (billions)*
Provided by the Dept. of Commerce, Bureau of Economic Analysis, the Current Account is released quarterly for the prior quarter. The current account balance measures net exports in goods and services, plus net earnings on overseas investments, plus cash transfers.

### Other Events FX Traders Must Pay Attention to

#### FOMC meetings
The Federal Open Market Committee, the group within the U.S. Federal Reserve Bank that manages the Fed Funds rate, and monetary policy. The FOMC meets eight times per year.

#### ECB Governing Council meetings
The Governing Council is the group within the European Central Bank responsible for setting the main REFI interest rate for Euro zone, and managing monetary policy. The Governing Council meets ten times a year.

# Index

Arab oil embargo, 8
Asia, 7, 20, 21, 37
Asian currency crises, 11
Balance of payments, 14, 16, 49, 58
BIS, 10, 49
Bretton Woods Conference, 6, 54
Call, 30, 49
Capital flows, 3, 7, 15, 17, 28, 37, 44
Central bank, 6, 7, 11, 12, 14, 16, 37, 44, 48, 49, 51, 52, 53, 56, 57, 58
China, 10, 13, 57
CitiFX Pro, 21, 39
CME, 29, 53
Control risk, 40, 42
Convertible, 3
Correlation, 23
Correlation coefficients, 23
Credit risk, 40
Cross currency, 26
Cyprus, 3, 11
Day trader, 2, 14, 18, 21, 22, 23, 27, 31, 32, 33, 34, 37, 38, 39, 41, 42, 43, 44, 45, 57
Dodd-Frank, 20, 39
EBS, 21
e-Commerce, 21
ETF's, 1
Euro area, 9, 17, 51
Euro currency, 9
Europe, 7, 8, 9, 10, 20, 21, 37, 52
xchange rate determination, 2
Financial risk, 34, 40, 41

Foreign currency, 2, 17, 30
Foreign exchange, 1, 2, 3, 5, 7, 12, 13, 16, 17, 18, 19, 20, 21, 24, 26, 29, 30, 33, 34, 35, 37, 40, 41, 42, 43, 49, 53, 56, 58, 59
Forward, 24, 27, 28, 29, 30, 31, 40, 51, 57, 59
France, 5, 7, 10, 11
Fundamental analysis, 14
futures, 1, 29, 31, 40
FX brokers, 1, 18, 22, 38, 44, 45, 55
FXCM, 21, 39
G5, 10
G7, 11
GDP, 66
Germany, 7, 9, 10, 11
Globex, 29
Gold Pool, 7
Gold standard, 5, 6, 8, 20
Greece, 11
Hot money, 3, 16
International Monetary Fund (IMF), 6
Japan, 9, 10, 11, 12, 15, 49
Latin Monetary Union, 5
Law of One Price, 15
Leverage, 1, 39, 41, 45, 55
Limit orders, 34, 38, 47
London, 16, 20, 54
Margin account, 1, 43, 45, 46
Middle East, 10, 37
New York, 16, 20, 21, 31, 64
New Zealand, 21, 24
Nixon, 9
Nostro, 32

Operational risk, 40, 42
Options, 29, 30, 31, 39, 40, 44, 49,
    51, 59
Paul Volker, 10
Purchasing Power Parity, 15
Put, 31, 57
Reuters, 21
Risk management, 2, 34, 42, 53
S/L, 35, 36, 47, 59
Smithsonian Agreement, 9
Special Drawing Rights, 10, 12, 58

Spot trade, 24
T/P, 35, 36, 47, 59
Technical analysis, 18, 19, 38, 44
Thailand's, 11
The Plaza agreement, 10
Tokyo, 15, 16, 20
Treasury International Capital flow,
    16
U.S. Congress, 51
Value dates, 24

# References

Frank, H. Robert, & Bernanke, S. Ben (2009). *Principles of Economics*. New York, NY: McGraw-Hill Irwin.

*Foreign Exchange and money market operations*. (1992). Switzerland: SBC.

Investopedia online. http://www.investopedia.com/search.

Made in the USA
San Bernardino, CA
29 December 2017